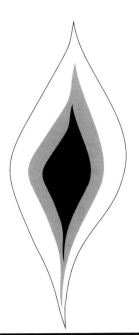

POWER FROM THE SUN

Susan Bullen

Other titles in this series include:
Power from the Earth
Power from Plants
Power from Water
Power from the Wind

Cover: Solar dishes used to trap energy from the Sun.

Editor: Deb Elliott

Designer: David Armitage

Text is based on *Solar Energy* in the Alternative Energy series published in 1990.

Picture acknowledgements
David Bowden 10; Chapel Studios 4; Mary Evans Picture Library 11; Eye Ubiquitous 16,20; Jimmy Holmes 19; Neste Advanced Power Systems 22; National Power 26; Oxfam 21 (bottom); Science Photo Library 12,13; Topham Picture Library 21 (top); US Department of Energy 25 (both); Wayland Picture Library 6,23; Zefa Picture Library 4,5,7,9,14,19. All artwork is by Nick Hawken.

First published in 1993 by
Wayland (Publishers) Limited
61 Western Road, Hove, East Sussex BN3 1JD

© Copyright Wayland (Publishers) Limited

British Library Cataloguing in Publication Data
Bullen, Susan
Power from the Sun. - (Energy Series)
I. Title II. Series
333.792

ISBN 0 7502 0721 3

Typeset by Perspective Marketing Limited

Printed in Italy by G.Canale & C.S.p.A.

Contents

We need energy

We all need energy. It's like an invisible
force inside us that makes our bodies
work. We get our energy from eating
food, and we use it up as we move
around. You will use up some energy
just by reading this book!

Drilling for oil in Indonesia

*Sunbathers enjoying heat
from the Sun.*

An Australian coal mine.

Machines also need energy to make them work. Most of them run on electricity. This is made by burning coal, oil and gas. These are fossil fuels. They are traces of living things found on Earth millions of years ago.

There are millions and millions of machines in the world. They need lots of electricity and are using up the world's fossil fuels.

Energy from the Sun

Coal, oil and gas will not last forever. When they run out, we will need other energy sources. We can make electricity from the power of the wind, from ocean waves and from mountain streams. But there is a much greater source of energy – the Sun.

This is a bush fire. Burning trees are giving out energy they once took in from the Sun.

The Sun controls our weather – the wind, clouds and rain.

The Sun gives our planet heat and light. All plants and animals need energy from the Sun to live.

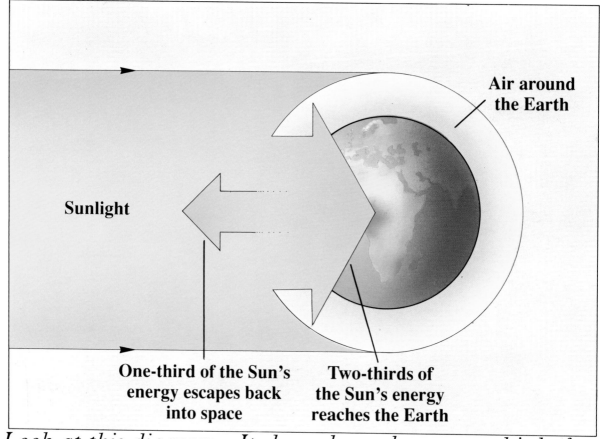

Look at this diagram. It shows how almost one-third of the Sun's energy escapes back into space.

The Sun is like a giant fireball, over 100 times bigger than planet Earth. On the Sun there are two gases – hydrogen and helium. These cause huge explosions, which give out powerful rays of heat and light.

These rays travel from the Sun towards Earth. Almost one-third escapes into space along the way. The rest reach our planet as heat and light energy.

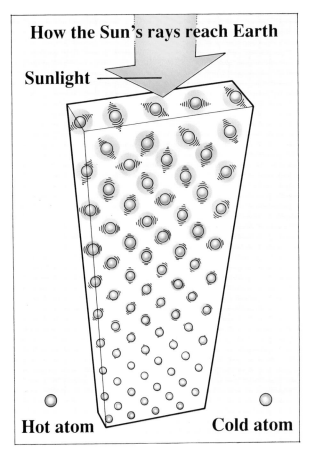

How the Sun's rays reach Earth

Sunlight

Hot atom   Cold atom

This diagram shows how the Sun warms things up.

When the Sun's rays touch an object, tiny particles inside it called atoms move around very quickly. This makes the object warm.

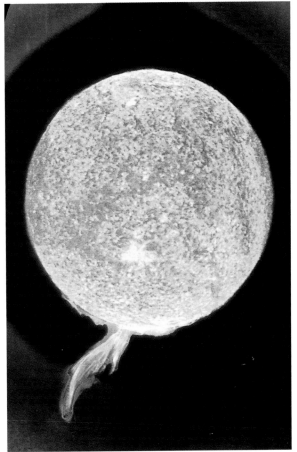

A huge jet of energy leaps from the Sun's surface. This is a solar flare.

Using the Sun's energy

Thousands of years ago, the first people learned how to dry animals' skins and food plants in the warmth of the Sun. Over time, people discovered that homes were warmer if they faced the Sun for much of the day. Many crops grow better on sunny slopes.

A simple water heater.

Glass top

Black lining

Silk drying in the Sun.

Using the power of the Sun to work a printing press in 1882 in France.

About 300 years ago, a Swiss scientist built a water heater that used the Sun's energy. It was a wooden box with a glass top and a black base. The black part absorbed the Sun's heat and made the water very hot.

In the 1800s, the French used the Sun's rays to boil water for steam-powered printing presses.

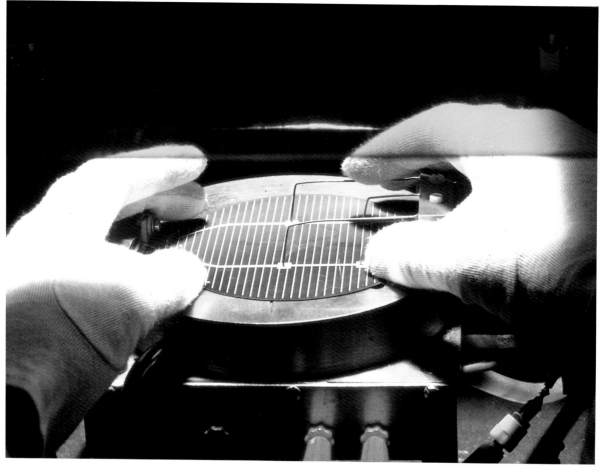

A multicoloured solar cell. You can see the wires that cover it.

Energy from the Sun is called solar power.
We can use solar cells to trap this energy.
The small cells are covered with fine wires.
These pick up electricity made by sunlight.
We use solar cells to power small everyday
objects like watches and calculators.

A man in China using solar cells to power his television.

It is less easy to use solar power for larger items and machines. This is because many solar cells are needed and they take up a lot of room. Also, the Sun is not always shining, for example at night or in winter.

A large field of solar collectors. Some people think they are ugly.

Solar power is free and does not cause pollution. But it is expensive to make the solar cells and collectors that trap the sunlight. Also these solar collectors take up a lot of land. But solar power will be very important in the future.

One day, people may build solar chimneys. These are tall chimneys under a large plastic roof.

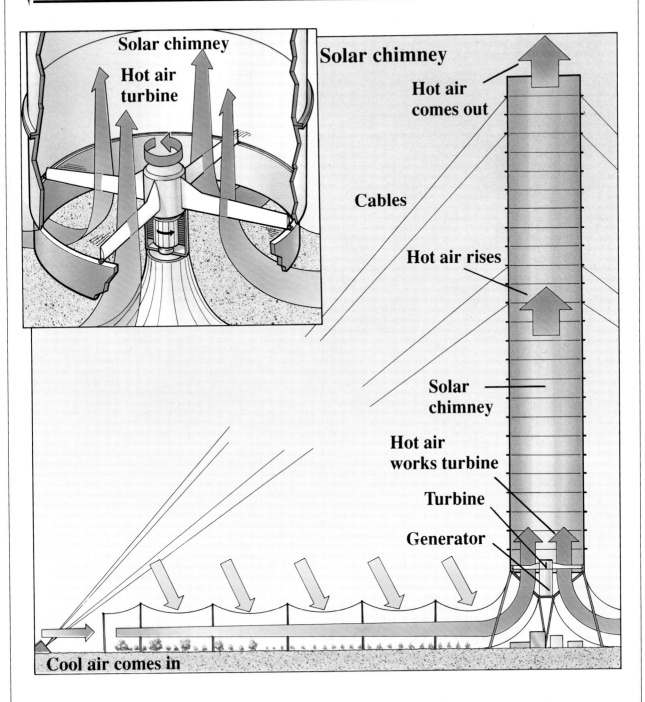

Solar chimney

Hot air turbine

Solar chimney

Hot air comes out

Cables

Hot air rises

Solar chimney

Hot air works turbine

Turbine

Generator

Cool air comes in

The Sun's rays would pass through the clear plastic and warm up the air. The hot air would rise up the chimneys and drive a turbine to make electricity.

Heat from the Sun

Some houses have a glass wall to let in more sunlight.

When sunlight passes through a window, it warms up a room. Some new houses have a wall of glass with a black material behind it. The dark colour takes up more of the Sun's heat and keeps the house warm for many hours.

In sunny countries, people often use sunshine to make hot water for their homes. They put solar panels on their roofs. These take up energy from the Sun during the daytime. The heat warms up water in a tank or in pipes that touch the solar panels.

This kind of solar panel is used on houses in sunny countries.

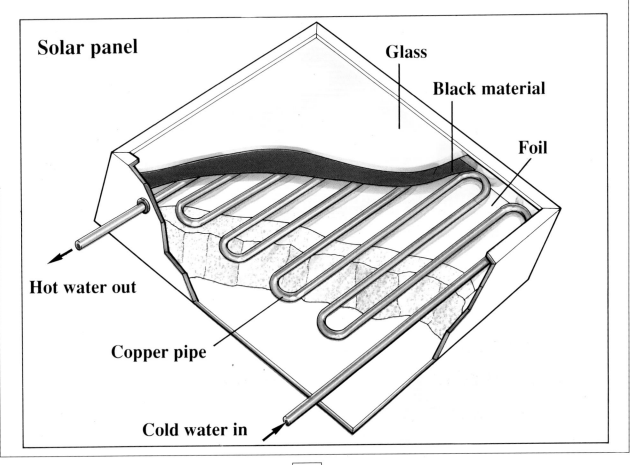

Solar panel

Glass

Black material

Foil

Hot water out

Copper pipe

Cold water in

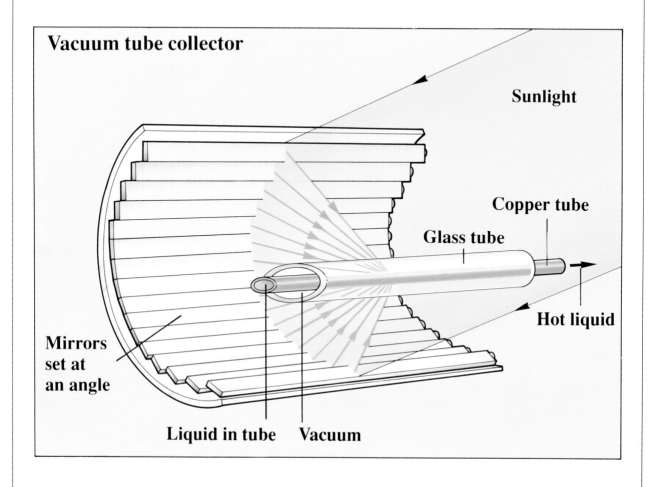

Vacuum tube collector

Sunlight

Copper tube

Glass tube

Hot liquid

Mirrors
set at
an angle

Liquid in tube   Vacuum

On the last page you saw a simple solar panel. The
diagram above shows a vacuum tube collector. The
tube has no air inside it, so all the heat it collects
cannot escape. This makes very hot water - much
hotter than you need in your bath!

Water in this pot heats up as the Sun's rays are bounced on to it from the curved reflector below.

These roofs in Israel are covered in solar panels.

There are other kinds of heat collectors. Some are shiny and curved. They bounce back the Sun's rays in a strong beam on to tubes of water. This heats up the water inside. People can use curved dish reflectors to cook food or to boil a pot of water.

Electricity from sunlight

You have read how we use the Sun's heat to make energy. But we can also use the Sun's light to make electricity. To do this, people use solar cells made from silicon. The silicon cells make electricity when they are hit by sunlight.

Solar cells provide electricity for people in high mountain villages.

Above *This is a panel of solar cells. They are light and easy to transport.*

Below *Solar cells make the electricity for this water pump in Africa.*

Each cell only makes a small amount of electricity. So plenty of them are needed at one time. Solar cells are very useful in remote places like villages in mountains or deserts. They make enough electricity to power telephones and water pumps.

Solar cells are very light. They can be taken to remote villages. They can even be carried by people on the move, so they can have power wherever they go.

This desert camel is carrying a solar-powered refrigerator. It can keep food or medicines cold in the desert.

A large solar power station in California, USA.

We can make a lot of electricity from the Sun at large solar power stations. These can supply electricity for all the homes in a small town.

Solar power – today and always

Solar power stations can make electricity by using steam power. They use many mirrors to reflect the Sun's rays on to a large boiler with oil inside it. The oil becomes so hot, it turns water into steam. The steam drives a turbine and this makes electricity.

How a steam-driven turbine works.

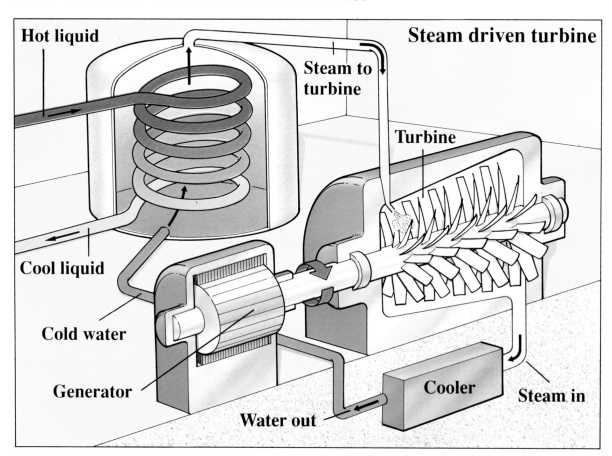

Hot liquid — Steam driven turbine — Steam to turbine — Turbine — Cool liquid — Cold water — Generator — Water out — Cooler — Steam in

The tower and mirrors of Solar One.

Solar One is a large solar power station in California, USA. It has a tall tower with a boiler and many mirrors around it on the ground. The boiler makes the steam to make electricity.

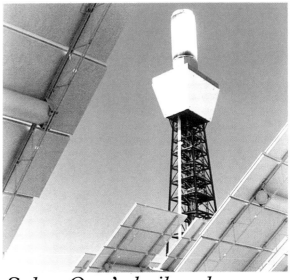

Solar One's boiler glows white-hot.

Thousands of mirrors cover the huge wall at Odeilo.

The solar furnace at Odeilo in France has a wall of mirrors. They point the Sun's rays at a tower with a furnace inside.

Solar power would be more useful if we could store it. A solar pond can store the Sun's heat long after the Sun has stopped shining. The pond has a black lining which keeps in the Sun's heat.

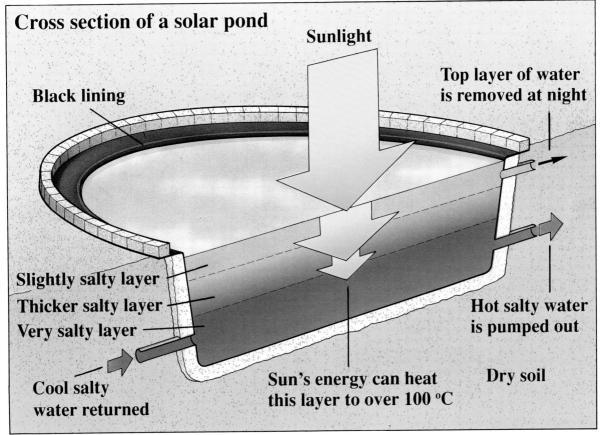

Cross section of a solar pond

Sunlight

Black lining

Top layer of water is removed at night

Slightly salty layer
Thicker salty layer
Very salty layer

Hot salty water is pumped out

Cool salty water returned

Sun's energy can heat this layer to over 100 °C

Dry soil

Solar ponds store warm water heated by the Sun.
This can be used at night or on dull days.

You have seen that there are many ways of using power from the Sun. Solar power is clean and helps provide the energy we need. Coal oil and gas will run out one day but the Sun will keep on shining.

Make a solar barbecue

You need

a strong cardboard box, a piece of very thick cardboard, rubber cement, aluminium foil, sticky tape, thick metal wire (a straightened coat hanger is ideal), two nuts and bolts, a pre-cooked sausage, such as a frankfurter.

What to do

1 Cut the top and one side out of the box. This makes the frame of your solar cooker.

2 Use the thick cardboard and cut a circle of about the same size as the height of your box. Now cut the circle in half. Cut a strip of card slightly shorter than the length of the box, and wide enough to fit around the curved edges of the half-circles.

3 Use the rubber cement to glue the foil to one side of each half-circle. Glue foil to one side of the strip of card.

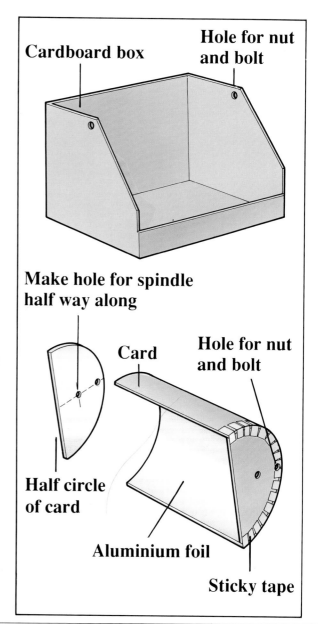

Cardboard box

Hole for nut and bolt

Make hole for spindle half way along

Card

Hole for nut and bolt

Half circle of card

Aluminium foil

Sticky tape

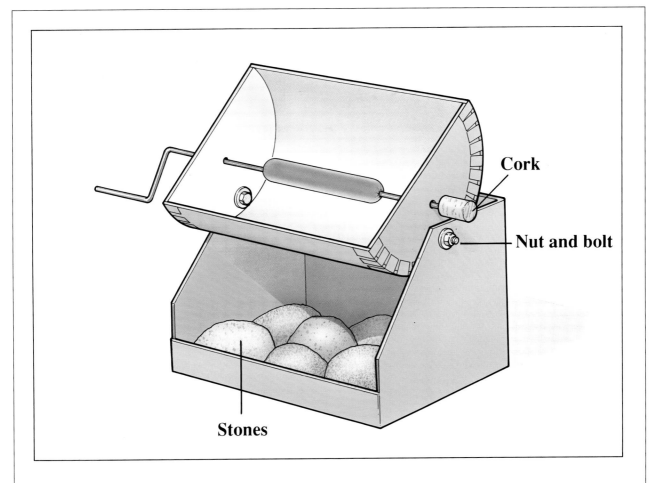

Cork

Nut and bolt

Stones

4 Tape each end of the card to one of the half-circles. The foil should face inwards. You have now made a curved reflector. Fix this to the frame with the nuts and bolts. Use the diagram to help you.

5 Make a hole in each end of the reflector. Pass the thick wire through this. Put stones in the bottom of the box to make it more stable.

6 Pull the wire spindle halfway out of the reflector. Thread on a frankfurter sausage and push the spindle through the hole again.

7 Point your barbecue towards the Sun. As the sausage browns, turn the spindle handle, so it cooks evenly. The frankfurter will cook more quickly on a sunny summer day.

Glossary

Atmosphere The layer of gases that surrounds the Earth.

Atoms All things are made up of thousands of atoms. The atoms themselves are too small to be seen.

Furnace A very hot kind of oven used to melt metals.

Gases Light airy substances. There are gases in the air but we cannot see them.

Oxygen A gas in the air we breathe. Most gases cannot be seen.

Pollution Harming the environment with strong chemicals, smoke or litter.

Reflect To bounce something back. A mirror reflects the Sun's rays.

Reflector A curved dish with mirrors that reflects the Sun's rays.

Remote Hidden away and difficult to get to.

Silicon A substance found in sand and rock. It is used to make solar cells.

Solar This word means 'from the Sun'.

Steam Water becomes steam when it boils and turns into a fine mist of tiny droplets.

Turbine A machine like a propeller. It turns around to drive a generator, which makes electricity.

Vacuum An empty space that has no air inside it.

Books to read

Energy by Deborah Elliott (Wayland, 1993)

Light by Graham Peacock and Terry Hudson (Wayland, 1993)

My Science Book of Energy by Neil Ardley (Dorling Kindersley, 1992)

Power by Julie Brown and Robert Brown (Belitha Press, 1991)

Index